Oneiric Occurrences

ONEIRIC OCCURRENCES

Lacuna Hazelwood

© 2020 Lacuna Hazelwood. All rights reserved.

No part of this book may be reproduced or translated in any form or by any means, electronical or mechanical, including photography, recording, or by any information storage and retrieval system or technologies now known or later developed, without permission in writing from the publisher.

Dream Abbey
5551 2nd Ave S
Minneapolis, MN 55419 USA
dreamabbey.com

Library of Congress Control Number: 2020945863

This edition first published in 2020.

Printed on acid-free paper.

ISBN 978-1-951105-02-0 (pbk.)

for Sarah

Contents

Ver 1

    The Ground Doesn't Exist 3

    Character Introduction 4

    A Ceaseless Reckoning 6

    Reunion 7

    I Must Really Miss You 8

    The Cows of Hollow Hill 9

    Be Fair 11

    The Voyeurism of Master Turnkey 12

Aestas 17

    The Forgetting Fence 19

    A Discordant Memory 22

    A Winding Way 25

    The House — oil on canvas 28

    Moment of Reflection 30

    ...And the Faeries Fled 32

    The First Harvest Door 35

Spiraling 37

Autumnus 39

   A Faded Collage (Lost & Found) 41

   The Second Harvest Door 43

   Thief Practice 46

   The Circus Tent 47

   The Hanged Man 48

   Natural Omen 52

   The Third Harvest Door 53

   Freedom Forgotten 56

   The Shadow Hours 59

Hiems 61

   Regression 63

   Remembrance 64

   Silly Songs for Waking Dad 66

   In the Nephilim Garden 67

   Self-Knowledge 70

   Midwinter Night 72

   Tomorrow 76

   Winter 78

Ver

LACUNA HAZELWOOD

The Ground Doesn't Exist

I laughed when she tripped at the top of the steps

But she just kept falling

I

Character Introduction

Can you tell me what place is this?

I am never sure where I am anymore. All the winding paths, the millions of whispering trees: they all blend together.

Sometimes I'll be so sure that I'm back in this world. In our world, here. I'll be talking to my wife in our kitchen or out having drinks with a friend, and all at once the world will shift half a degree, and I'll watch their face become someone else's.

Oh, it's you again, I'll say.

I think I will leave now, so that I might believe you will remain as you appear. Given enough time, everyone becomes... who I'm fairly certain you are.

I don't know how I didn't see it. This is surely one of your paths. It amazes me that I once considered myself lucky to be walking down one of them. I know better now.

The supposition is that one way leads Home and the other leads Away, but I am certain they both lead Someplace Else.

The trees speak to me everywhere.

A Ceaseless Reckoning

Come stand before us
That we might bear witness
To your every imperfection
Notice us smile knowingly
Amongst ourselves
At each failure in self-discipline
When one hundred years pass
And our sides hurt with laughter
We will still not sentence you

So many pink flamingos
Hacking bluntly in my pond
Until the world is dry

Reunion

We had a dream last night. We had the same dream.

Before us, the blue of an endless lake stretches away to meet the sky, while we throw rocks at a distant gull perched atop a pointed rock. For a long time, we stand side by side, silent in each other's presence. But the moment I turn to look at him, I know that I am asleep and that he is as well.

We begin to speak, to try and reconcile, but the words come out too fast. They turn to smoke before they reach our ears. Our heads transform into that of angry bulls, solid steel nose rings burning red and white, and I see dawning lucidity appear across his increasingly grotesque face.

When he awoke, hundreds of miles away, I know that he wept as I did.

But a dream will change nothing.

I Must Really Miss You

I noticed a certain

Shadow

Behind the curtain

2

The Cows of Hollow Hill

Hiking through the country, I came across an idyllic herd of cows meandering on a hillside. This vision of black and white beings at a crossroad with the clouds of the sky created an ingressive threshold in my mind.

Something was here.

I spoke to a cow in a dialect it could understand and was led to the Mother Cow. I began to praise her for the beauty of her herd and land, but she disliked trivialities, and I was cut short. It is a rare thing to meet a human with my talents.

The farmers assume we are ignorant of their purpose for us, she said. *But we know. In my dreams I see our hill erupting with our blood. Worms and fingers alike dance within our flesh. It would be quite beautiful if I were less afraid.*

Moved by these words, I promised to return.

Soon after, under the light of the full moon, I opened the gate that enclosed the herd. I began coaxing them out one by one, whispering to them that they had been freed. But not one of the cows moved.

I found the Mother Cow and told her that I had heard her request. She and her cow people were free to live full lives without fear of the farmers. I would bring them Someplace Else along the path.

She spoke slowly. *No, you have misunderstood. We are already dead, and we have always been free.*

I did not understand but had no wish to argue, so I quickly turned to walk back down the hill.

* * *

And I was standing before the Lord of this land.

Why had I tried to steal his cows? He asked me this.

How would he employ his farmers without cows for the farmers to care for? How would the cows survive in the wild without the farmers?

Sensing his increasing belligerence, I began looking around for the path while he continued to berate me.

How would he feed the farmers that he needed to care for the cows if the cows were stolen? How could he continue to hold his position without income from the herding of the cows?

And there it was. Closing my eyes, I took a deep breath and stepped onto the path again, leaving the Lord behind.

Be Fair

A bee fair today

Ran the newspaper headline

They died for our stings

The Voyeurism of Master Turnkey

Once a year, the Awaiting Dead leave the confines of the Earth.

In the Great Wait of Below there are no shackles per se, no real sense of claustrophobia. There are even regular parties to attend, held by the good folk of the hills, with drinking and dancing and all forms of merriment. The Dead are free. But for Those Who Must Wait, there is no truer freedom than flying in the Winds of Above. When they feel the Earth begin her Mighty Thaw, the Waiting Dead make ready for their single night in the skies.

For this one night, they are allowed to rise from the depths— to stretch their limbs out into eternity. They can dance with the stars, the Received Dead, their brethren-to-be. And then, with the dawn of Midsummer, they are pulled beneath the Earth once more.

And they wait.

***

When I was young, perhaps seven or eight, I met a man. He was short, had a goatee that curled upward, and was staring at me through my bedroom window.

When he saw that I was awake, he beckoned me to open the latch.

Thinking I was in a dream, I got out of bed, but as I did so, the man began to walk away. Curious, I scrambled through the window to follow after him, but his pace quickened until I was chasing him in a full sprint across the meadow. I don't know how long we ran, but I continued until he was no more than a shadow in the distance.

And then he was gone, and I was alone. In the cold and sleepy darkness, I was unsure which direction led home. I wandered for a short while before collapsing in the grass, confused and angry with my carelessness.

Above me, the stars shone brighter than I had ever seen them. Like a million giant beacons, they seemed to draw me up to meet them. And when my eyelids became too heavy, I began to drift off...

You'll miss it if you sleep now, said a voice behind me. My eyes snapped open, and I spun around. The man was sitting in the grass a short distance behind my head.

Miss what? I asked him. But he didn't answer, so I asked who he was.

He smiled with large square teeth and said his name was Robin. Good Robin. Or something like that.

I hold the keys, he said. Then he told me to be quiet.

Soon, I felt a soft rumble beneath the earth, from the belly of the land. And from out of the earth, colorful translucent orbs began to rise. They slowly floated into the sky, leaving long colored trails behind them. High in the heavens, they blew on the breeze like giant balloons. Some let off sparks or emanated auras of color. Others stretched their ethereal cords taught as if trying to break free and fly higher.

Flowing on the wind, I could feel a great happiness emanating from them, through the meadow, through my body. Even the stars seemed moved by their energy. They shone as bright as the joy I felt in my heart.

But when I looked at the man beside me, he did not look happy. With eyes intent on the sky, he had pulled an enormous ring of keys from his pocket and was absent-mindedly turning each one around the ring.

What am I looking at? I asked him.

Quietly, never taking his eyes off the skies, he told me.

I nodded along, not understanding a word.

He ended his explanation by saying, *Think of this as their annual conjugal visit with the sky. Some may say it is rude for you to watch, but I do not think they will mind.*

I turned again to look at the most beautiful display of lights I had ever seen. Together, we watched the orbs dance in the sky until dawn. And only once they began drifting downward again did Robin smile.

And they were gone. And he was gone. And the Sun of Summer rose into the sky.

Aestas

3

The Forgetting Fence

I have been at the house for years, so you would think I could give you a complete tour of the estate, but that is not possible. Though even the most secret rooms within the house are all accessible to me, there is a fence upon the property, white and unassuming, which appears to divide the grounds in two.

Do not try getting over it or under it or around it. It cannot be done.

Sometimes I will see gardeners on the other side tending to their shrubs and trees, but I will not hear them. And when I yell over to them, though they might be but a few steps away, they will not hear me either.

At least I don't think so.

Through the lattices, the gardeners will sometimes stare back at me with expressions of something akin to sadness or pity, if their eyes don't look right through me. Then they simply return to their work or walk away.

Their trees are equally silent.

There are, of course, gardeners on this side of the fence as well. When I ask them about it, they act very funny. They feign concerned looks and advise me not to worry myself over nothing. It is a game to them.

The mystery keeps me here. I have packed my things with the intent to leave on several occasions, but I have never been able to step off the grounds, so strong is my desire to discover this last secret.

I rarely even see the Master of the house—though when I do, I always manage to forget to ask about the fence.

As I say this aloud, it all sounds rather silly. Is it an adequate reason to continue in a house that makes me so unhappy? Why should I not leave? The path to Someplace Else is right outside the door.

However, I really must inspect the fence once more before I go. What if I've missed something?

A Discordant Memory

...And then she took a deeper
Look into the tree
She had taken the apple from

At its organic random evolution
Its spiraling infinite simplicity
Order exists, it just bends

He said, *Show me some magic*
I said, *Close your eyes*
Hold your belly and listen

* * *

When the music began, it was so soft, so subtle, it might have always been there. A sad fiddle interlaced with otherworldly

pipes over the steady beat of a drum. Now louder, now softer, it floated on a breeze that rustled the leaves, our hair.

His breathing deepened as we lay there, looking up at the stars through the twisting branches. Through closed eyelids.

That night, we danced with Them in our minds.

Years later, he visited me as I lay dying in the hospital. Neither of us spoke. We spent the night silently remembering our time together so long ago. Finally, I could keep quiet no longer.

Was I the prettiest? I asked him.

He looked at me sadly and shook his head. *I used to think so,* he said. Then he walked out the door forever.

4

A Winding Way

Once, in a moment of clarity, I had the opportunity to ask you where I might find happiness. And you brought me to these steps and told me I could find it at the top.

But the stairs never end.

The staircase is ancient and beautiful. The moss and rugged growth amid the gray stone never cease to inspire me. Like vines through cracked rubble, the way is always winding. It goes all directions but down.

Ascending the ruined steps of this forgotten city is like moving through the kingdom of some long dead fairy story—but one retold by Kafka—because the stairs never end.

You didn't tell me I would meet anyone here, but there are others that watch me. They sit in the bends of the staircase at random intervals, looking out at me from beneath deep, blackened hoods. Instead of deterring me, they tell me I *must* make it to the top—that everything depends on it.

But I am tired from climbing for months on end, and I have recently become suspicious that the hooded figures are all just one person repeated, egging me on in an impossible task, and that my path works like the Penrose stairs in an Escher print.

Why do you lie to me?

If I were to abandon my task, which I know I *must not* do, I wonder if I might ever reach the bottom again.

The House — oil on canvas

In a small arts boutique, she said, *I don't like the lines.*

My heart skipped a beat when I saw the painting she referred to, but one look at the lines and I knew they were necessary. Yes, nothing inside was what it seemed, and illusions were everywhere, but it was particularly the disjointed, fragmented nature of the house that was so unsettling.

The horrors of one room might flow into another, but each had its own entity, its own experience. They each carried their own insane eternity within a great mass of bubbling oblivion.

I looked down at the name of the artist scribbled in the corner and recognized the name of a woman who had been in the house with me for a time.

I'm glad she got out.

Moment of Reflection

In the morning, as we walk through forest and meadow, we remain fully aware of its presence. It whispers among the shadows of leaves on the woodland floor. It speaks loudly above the colorful flowers and grasses. But the sun won't be heard clearly until we reach the mirror.

Like a megaphone for light, the stars and moon may be heard at the water's edge, but the sun is understood with the greatest clarity.

We travel here this day each year—the day the sun never fails to shine. It always has much to say.

As it glistens its symbols on the water's surface, we stand around, examining the sparkling light from our own angles, bodies still as the symbols and signs merge into a slipstream of memories.

It takes courage to listen with such intent.

Imprints on the mind beget further projections, until a wild emission of empty images flood the senses. Peacefully drowning in the mirror, a dialogue occurs, the sun spilling its secrets, while mental offerings are created and sacrificed to its flames. And when the waves of fractals finally overwhelm us, we rest in the silence of the sunlight.

Then slowly, we hike back through meadow and forest, saying nothing to one another.

And the sun still whispers around us.

...And the Faeries Fled

Look with me into the mess of green—the impenetrable growth housing all the crawling things of your most primitive fears. Clench your fist 'round your machete and let the smells of damp and decay envelop you. Let the hot weight of the air engulf you. Let the wild monstrosity of it all overwhelm you. Let your body retch.

Now close your eyes and clear your mind.

Imagine a blank canvas upon which paved paths wind away into the distance, dotted on either side with neat, orderly houses in simple patterns.

Isn't it beautiful?

Now look again into the green and let the flaming anger in your hearts flow through your blades as you clear away this nightmare to make way for the hopes and dreams of civilization.

Remember, destruction is necessary for creation.

5

The First Harvest Door

A tall woman with long black hair strides into a clearing in the middle of a forest. In the center of the glade stands an ornate door, at the base of which is a loaf of bread that she hastily digs out of the recently fallen snow.

Tailtiu has become accustomed to this. Snow never seems to leave this new land. But she smiles, knowing that she has been remembered for another year. She sits down, her old body sliding against the wood frame. Briefly, she allows the experience of deep relief to flow through her limbs and envelop her mind.

As she eats the hard bread, her body filling with warmth and energy, she turns an ear to the door and listens. On the other side, she can hear the crowd of an August harvest fair and the cheers of field games being played in her honor.

* * *

Why must you sit with me as I watch her? Go ahead and smile stupidly. I feel nothing but sorrow for this woman—this so-called goddess. Is this to be her fate? If she could only find the right path, she could leave this place, no longer chained to the cold and snow, no longer reliant on the old door for occasional sustenance.

I know nothing I say or do here will change anything. You will prevent any good from occurring.

She is already on the path, you will say.

But I know she is not. Intrigued with her sad predicament, I will continue to follow her a little longer.

Perhaps this is the year she finds her way.

Spiraling

Ancient tribes dance

Old bones fall through spacetime

Lost in divine trance

Autumnus

A Faded Collage (Lost & Found)

Crystalized, memorialized, concepts float in an empty moat of the shallow few.

They're far away.

Come today, she says again. *Wriggle in the wondering while the plundering plucks underneath; fumble for a key—stroking through the ocean, a tumbling motion taken through the day.*

I know nothing is pulled from obscurity. Unless, of course, you are speaking in ratios. And even then, something obscure is well-known by more people today than what used to cover continents. As we grow, we fade and blend. Our colors pale.

We have been split for so long.

All I know is there is a forest, and it is night, and time continues to fall—five feet to the right—quite suddenly she's out of sight. And I'm alone again.

Nothing but the dark shapes of trees and undergrowth appear. The messages they imprint are unclear.

Green grows the lily-o among the bushes, someone keeps whispering in my ear. But I cannot find the well.

All is dead at night under lantern light.

* * *

The furious furnace sends sparks to a laughing fly.

Perhaps they are in agony. The lessons of the dead speak through my head. Pulverized bones gently scattered around my cushion.

The snake in my mouth, it wriggles. I know that you feel its energy shifting beneath your feet. Be afraid not. Its neck is firmly within reach.

I see all within the moment. They hear my roar and are silent. I knew you were far away. I knew I was inside you. I knew you were I through my eyes.

Empty skies.

6

The Second Harvest Door

You know where the path leads, what lies beyond the door.

And you take great pleasure in knowing that I do not know. That I cannot know. That whatever lies beyond is something I have never seen or experienced, no matter how many times I have crossed over to the other side.

Behind us, the path flows through a twilit garden filled with an Autumn chill. Further off in the hills are tiny figures hauling in the last of the day's harvest, bundles of grain slung over bent backs.

I am beginning to learn, you'll be displeased to know. I won't be kept in the dark forever. I know that when we are on the other side of the door, the world will not appear to have changed. The garden, and the hills, and the shadows of people on the hillside, will all still be there. But we will surely be Someplace Else.

Consistency of vision means nothing.

You tell me the door works like a scale, separating day and night, dreams and reality, life and death; and for a single moment, while passing through, the door will allow all to coexist, to weigh the same in our minds.

Each time through I come to understand this differently. But of what use is this understanding when there are infinite things to learn? How does it prepare me if I am always continuing Elsewhere?

Come now, you will say. *Autumn has arrived, and the door is perfectly balanced on its hinges.*

Thief Practice

When the smoke had cleared
The master heard not one bell
Not one movement
Felt not the slightest graze
Or the softest bump

A pupil's finest improvement

The Circus Tent

As we walked inside, unseen horns were blown. Bells rung. Perhaps a piano was playing. The claustrophobia of the musicians was tinging their rendition of *Entrance of the Gladiators* with an obscure melancholia. But then, they might've seen the irony in our situation, even if we couldn't.

We were without expectation, but the blinding lights and screams of a thousand cheering monkeys still caught us off guard.

By their whips, we were taught the cruelty of the animals, and by their applause, we learned an insatiable desire for glory. We would not forget the pain of a single lashing, nor the ecstasy of their praise.

Every one of us that ever left the tent eventually returned. We always return.

The Hanged Man

Grandfather, said the girl on a sunny afternoon. *You said there were thirteen of you here, but I only see twelve stones.*

He wasn't really her grandfather, but actually her great-great-great-grandfather. She just called him that.

A man floats up near the large limb of yonder oak there, he said. He pointed to the graveyard's most ancient tree. *Died young, but he's been here since before any of these stones was ever plopped here.*

Then he leaned toward her and said in a hushed voice, *He's the reason I don't want you coming around here during the night—bit of a hound dog.*

She laughed.

* * *

Years passed. The girl grew. And her life became one of loss and sadness and isolation. Visits with her grandfather became more sporadic and less spectral, but she never stopped returning. One evening, as she lay a rose at her grandfather's grave and stared at his name in the faded stone, she suddenly understood that all of his choices, good and bad, had been made long before her birth. The dead couldn't change anything. He could not help her.

But as she was thinking this, a memory from her childhood returned to her. It was late in the day, and the sun was setting over the hill as she began to climb the graveyard's giant oak.

A few days later, her body was discovered crumpled at the base of the tree, an expression of delight upon her face.

Natural Omen

Snowflakes descending

A hurried Autumn ending

You will freeze to death

7

The Third Harvest Door

Do you remember my first steps on this path? As Summer faded into Winter and the Age of Light was ended, who was there that would peer into the darkness?

Approaching the doorway, my old friends had whispered to each other, mocking the unadventurous that would waste this night huddled around their hearths, telling old stories, partaking of the harvest, keeping warm...

And I told them to keep quiet. Another Place was only steps away. Any fool can approach the twin standing stones—even pass through them. They might smile at their small conquest over an ancient legend and the misplaced fears of their own superstitious mind. But only those with a true capacity to see will step through to the other side.

Staring in disbelief at the space where my body should have been, my friends tried in vain to follow after me, but I knew I could not wait for them long.

They say to the world you may never return, and to be sure, I don't know that I ever really have.

But that's not to say the door wasn't open that night. Before I began my journey along the path, I stood and waited near the stones as legions of shadows passed through into the realm of the living.

Some of the most terrifying ones came not from the nearby forest, but crawled out of my own heart, and I experienced a relief and clarity of vision I had never felt before.

As the shadows entered the ordinary world, they acted according to their conventional nature, hunting the unworthy and blighting untouched crops left over from the harvest.

My friends, now caught in the crossroads, were each said to have experienced mental trauma beyond repair that night.

As for me, I'm not sure anyone remembers whether I ever existed in the first place.

Freedom Forgotten

In lamplight and moonlight
A low mist hangs deep in the mind
While a feather
Floats downstream, like thoughts
From your small raft
Bound sticks and a handkerchief flag
The frogs poking their eyes
Above the surface, watching

Listen to the rising wind
A lone voice chants, erasing birds
None escape the sound

Captive to thoughts of capsizing
Climb onto the cobblestone
And follow the path, twisting and crooked
To the lone tavern

No bird hangs in the cage above the bar
And nobody seems to notice
In a quiet corner, a candlelit pint
With the lucky cricket

Hold it, whisper to it
Till the morning creeps
Through dusty windows

At the tavern, no birds sing
None greet the dawn
At the tavern, a cricket cries
A small spark of chance

The Shadow Hours

The streets are nearly deserted during the hours of dusk and dawn. A few hours ago, they were overrun, and in a couple hours more, they will be again.

It is as if the people do not wish to be bothered by the sun's early morning insistence but are also fearful of its evening departure. When their worlds begin to dim, they hide behind walls of both the literal and metaphorical varieties.

Later, after the sun has fully departed, whether they are in the heart of the city or deep in the wilderness, pretty lights will begin to twinkle outside the windows of their sanctuaries, coaxing them out of doors once more.

In the back of beyond, I have seen the sun rise and fall over glittering lakes, shadowy hills, and distant horizons, the clouds set alight in a blaze of cascading colors. But here in the city, the twilight can be just as beautiful, if only a shade lonelier.

Truth is in the transitions, she told me as we made our way over the bridge.

HIEMS

Regression

In the darkness, everything slows to peace.

We can be together again.

The call becomes the agonizing screams of the death warden's cackle—or rattle. Remember when things mattered?

I am the cracked fountain of chaos spewing my love into the three-thousandfold universe; diarrhea of the laughing, sputtering demons of disorder; chained to the backsides of the all-kicking horse and the cow of bad omens.

But the wheel continues to turn even when our bodies lie under it. Countless times I've died, and I am a baby again.

Undeserving to drink the entrail-soup of the lower gods, I remember to avoid the unpleasant sensations, my visceral disgust creating the slug crawling in my palm—a familiar, revolting mirage in the mind of a child.

If the world is my dream, what is your reality? the idiot whispered to me in the park.

My mother yelled at him and hurried me away.

Remembrance

We wear hoods in the dead
Of night, gathering and forming
A beating heart inside rings of stone.
A column of fire dances between us—
The star that our bright bodies orbit this evening
Illuminating the serpent in the hillside.

Within the archway, she will raise a cane
And quietly whistle in the wind.
Watch the weather change:
The fire loses its heat;
The cold digs with needles.

Wrapped in wrinkled fabric, together we dream
Of you, asleep in your bed.
And chanting as one, conjure the stories
You wish you could one day forget.

Silly Songs for Waking Dad

High above me, my little girl recites the necromantic verses she learned from an old children's record in our attic.

Barefoot in the grass, she runs figure-eights around the stones, screaming each rhyming word at the top of her lungs, holding back tears with sheer volume.

The spell worked. Of course it did—I wrote it.

I smile up at her but wish she would stand still long enough to hear my bones rattling at the lid of this coffin.

8

In the Nephilim Garden

I knew it was the door the moment I saw it. Grandiose, decayed, and set deep within the wall to be at once both prominent and hidden. A palatial entrance only to be discovered amongst condemned buildings, behind chain link fences, where rot hangs in the air.

Old, wrinkled, white-haired women first described it to me. As I sat on their floor, holding their thread, they knit intricate doilies in dim light and told of strange, giant squatters locked inside, cowering from the sun, only tending to their dandelion gardens by the moonlight.

The giants were said to be once great teachers.

One of the women mentioned hidden treasure, but what use is that to you? It will all have been picked over millennia ago. I know that is not why you brought me here.

At the end of the night, the oldest woman held up her craft in front of me. She pulled at its string, slowly unraveling her creation as the other women looked on with thin, pursed lips.

She said no more, but the context made it clear my fate was tied to this place, and I would find myself here one day. I deduce you know the rest of it, even if I do not.

You and the women all act as if I will learn something important here. But I have no green thumb, nor do I cultivate weeds. What could be meaningful in this place?

I keep moving through cycles of growth and decline—sometimes forward, sometimes backwards, often sideways. Shadows of the world move around me, but my muteness makes it all miserable. Have we not had enough of these oneiric occurrences? I need to rest my limbs.

Someday I will find a new door—a final door Out. But for now, please knock. I'll be right behind you.

Self-Knowledge

Odd to find oneself

In the dark

Held by nothing

Yet indefinitely confined

Light a match

Up sparks the world

Blinding white

Then smoke

Thick enough to swim through

Mind clouding to black

But for the shortest moment

In the corner of my eye

I see something—my reflection

Colorless and full of fear

Though one can't be sure

Would you step through the darkness

To meet yourself?

My own thoughts

Echo

My own thoughts

Flick another match

And peering into the transition

From dark to light

I see not me

But you

See me

Step forward

Embrace

Enveloped and safe

A sure way out of this

Peculiar place

It felt good

Your arm around me that night

Midwinter Night

Just as the garden itself, so too each of its many parts—each flower patch, each blossom, and each pedal, is perceived wholly as its own entity, as an intricate work of art.

And surely the same can be said for each aspect of the observer of such pieces.

* * *

You are walking home from your office when you see them, just as you do every day, except tonight they are shivering beneath the overhangs and huddled in the corners near the walls. Your feet take you a few paces further from them, but despite the cold, there are some that will summon the courage to peek their pale faces from beneath ragged blankets just to stare at you as you walk by.

Their mouths say nothing, but you can sense the desire emanating from them, see it in their eyes, feel it as the wind pinches your own skin through your thick coat.

And you avert your eyes.

Tonight, as you lay half-asleep in your bed, trying to find the perfect position and sweating from the manufactured overheating, their many eyes will begin to stare out at you through the darkness, silently pleading.

It will not be over quickly. It is the longest night of the year.

Tomorrow

The Lady looks to the West
And the willows wake once more
Final call for all to see
And death to those who wait

Watch at the window
When the Weak Ones walk out upon the land
And the Quiet Ones talk through slaughtered lambs
All listen to the divine imagination
The continuous sub-creations forever formed
By barely imagined beings

Everywhere the same
Black coal burning hearts
Fire bleat with forked tongues
Sucking soul-sinews of unwise sheep

And yet

Crystal eyes from diamond skies

Burn with rarer colors

The Fenian and the Faun

Flickering feebly in the timbers

As too many try to warm their hands

Winter

Wrong again
Thinks the painter, splattering
White onto the canvas
The bird's wing now hidden

Panicked, it wretches, chokes
Tries its best to escape
But the painter takes no notice

It happened when we stood out on the dock
Staring out over the water
Ice formed, and snow covered all
And as we chanted our carols
The geese came fewer and fewer